THE

ULTIMATE FREEDOM

John H. Wyndham

MOUNTAINTOP
PUBLISHING

Mountaintop Publishing
4380 Highland Drive
Carlsbad, CA 92008
(760) 720-0000 fax (760) 729-1411
www. MountaintopPublishing.com

Printed in the United States of America
ISBN 0-9642628-0-0

Contents

Part I

Finding Freedom in Captivity

Chapter One

Chapter Two

Chapter Three

Part II

Breaking Out of Captivity in Freedom

Preface

Over the years interested people have asked about the book John H. Wyndham was writing prior to his passing in 1979. Although not finished in the strict sense of the word yet this little volume is complete and it falls naturally into an interesting pattern. First of all the author deals with his own experience, then broadens this to others around him and finally he speaks on a national and international level. This pattern is obvious in both Part I and Part II, and the reader should enjoy watching the ripple effect that one life can produce.

Perhaps the themes the book focuses on speak even more to today's world than when this work was written. Freedom, economics and spirituality engage the public's attention as never before and on a worldwide basis.

The fact that this writing does not take us further, into the author's later life, is probably of no real consequence as John Wyndham did not intend his book to be an autobiography. It begins with his war experience when the author is already in his mid-thirties with a wife and two small children. No, John Wyndham did not intend this to be an account of *his* life, but rather of the possibilities *of* life. He proved that there is a Science of Life, which is a spiritual rather than a physical science, and that this Science can be lived and learned. To help others live this spiritual and divine adventure was his goal. To this end, his book is being published.

A few biographical facts may be helpful to the reader. John Wyndham was a native of Holland who, while still a teenager, went to live with relatives in the United States of America. A few years later he made a new home in Australia. At the beginning of the Second World War he enlisted in the Royal Australian Air Force where, due to his native language of Dutch, he was made a liaison officer and sent to Indonesia, to the island of Java, before it fell to the Japanese. When they did overrun the island he and many others took refuge in private homes, and that is where his account begins. He does make reference now and then to the Javanese people, not to be confused with the Japanese who took over the island.

One added fact, before you join him in Java, might help you to understand the author. Whenever he recounted any of his wartime experiences to his family (and it was not often that he did) he would usually preface his remarks with a kindly, "When I was a guest of the Japanese." As his daughter, I can truly say that he did not impart the thought of resentment or that he had to deal with an enemy. He dealt with a thought world and a spiritual dimension for living.

Auriel Wyndham Livezey

Part I

Finding Freedom in Captivity

Part I

Finding Freedom in Captivity

Chapter One

CAPTURED!

It was dusk when I was captured. From the guest pavilion behind the house which had been my hiding place for the past several months, I watched as the big black sedan pulled up and a Japanese entered the gate. My only way of escape was over a wall at the end of the courtyard. As I made a leap for it, clasping the top of the wall and attempting to pull myself up, a shot rang out. Suddenly there was no way of escape.

The Ultimate Freedom

As we drove through the crowded streets in the sedan, I had a nostalgic glimpse of Bandung's suburban life, its rows of food stalls with their exotic smells of oriental cooking and the endless stream of colorfully dressed Javanese people carrying bundles on their heads or squatting around flickering oil lights to eat and talk. In minutes we reached the prison house, and the solid cell door closed behind me.

Through a barred window, facing a blank wall some six feet away, came the last glimmer of light. The cell was empty except for a wooden table. My first reaction was one of relief, for the tension I had felt during the months of hiding was gone. Curled up on the wooden table, I slept soundly that night.

With the coming of daylight came also the realization that I was in a situation where I could expect no outside help and was seemingly without any means of helping myself. Soon I was taken from my cell for interrogation. My passport (with military photo) and some of my other belongings had been found. The interrogation was abrupt and centered on my admitting that I was the

Captured!

officer in the passport picture and that a watch and other things belonged to me. Again, within just a few minutes, I was back in my cell.

Then came days and weeks in which I was left alone except for daily food which was handed in to me. You, dear reader, might understand that in this situation, fearing to be treated as a spy and executed, I turned to my only source for help — to God. Over past years the concept of God who loves His children had become somewhat familiar to me through reading the Scriptures with some regularity, together with a little Bible companion book giving the spiritual meaning of Scriptural sayings and events. How precious even a little knowledge of a loving ever-present God proves to be during such a time of trial! You see, as well as not seeing people or talking with anyone, I was not allowed to read. My request for a Bible was refused.

Then one day a civilian Japanese came to my cell door and showed me a diary in which I had written some philosophical thoughts on the future of the war predicting the defeat of the Japanese. This man gave me to understand that my plight was indeed serious as my fears had pictured.

I fell to my knees and prayed to God to be spared the experience of execution, promising that I would live my life to serve Him. Hope and a feeling of God's presence came as this prayer brought an immediate and clear direction. As if someone had spoken the words, there came the command, "Control thought."

There was no doubt in my mind but that this instruction came from God. This message was fully in accord with Jesus' teaching, "...when thou prayest, enter into thy closet, and when thou hast shut thy door, pray to thy Father which is in secret; and thy Father which seeth in secret shall reward thee openly" (Matt. 6:6).

Also from my Bible companion book I had learned that we must shut the door of our consciousness against evil suggestions in order that it may be open to the word of God. In short, I saw that controlling my thoughts meant praying. And praying that wasn't just asking God to do something for me, but praying that meant thinking truly, deeply, spiritually. From that moment,

Captured!

fearful suggestions, resentful suggestions, hateful suggestions were barred from entering my consciousness. When they came, and they came daily, hourly, and sometimes moment by moment, I absolutely refused to let them in. As these mental suggestions were kept out, divine thoughts began to flow into my consciousness. With a rusty old nail, I scratched the letters "C.T." on the wall of my cell as a constant reminder to control thought.

This true thinking had an immediate effect upon me — physically as well as mentally. My body felt little discomfort though there was only the stone floor or the wooden table to sleep or sit on, and the temperature varied from extreme heat during the day to the cold one experiences in tropical mountain regions at night.

The greatest wonder to me at that time was: How was it possible that God would help me for I considered myself such a sinner. Although I had accepted that God is loving, I had not yet grasped the meaning of what St. John says, that "God is Love." However, through my newfound thinking, a more spiritual sense of life was beginning to dawn on me. The battle was no longer with people and circumstances but with false thinking which was constantly being corrected and defeated by true thinking. The sense of time was eliminated. These weren't long days dragging on in endless uncertainty and unhappiness, but rather periods filled with new glimpses of what life really is, that Life is God and that man individually expresses this divine Life.

Oh, yes, my mental struggles were at times severe, especially when I let the grimness of my empty cell, the barred window, and the occasional sounds of wailing impress themselves on me. Nevertheless, it was daily becoming more apparent to me that my real life was not in, or dependent on, a physical body, nor at the mercy of adverse or cruel circumstances. This life, I saw, could not be destroyed. I glimpsed the truth of the Biblical statement, "In him (that is, in God) we live, and move, and have our being" (Acts 17:28).

Gradually a deep sense of peace and calm assurance descended on me. I remembered other comforting Bible statements, such as the one from Isaiah (26:3), "Thou wilt keep him in perfect

Captured!

peace, whose mind is stayed on thee:..." Wasn't this what controlling thought and keeping out false thoughts was all about — having our mind stayed on God? Then came parts of that beautiful 23rd Psalm, affirming trust in God's providence. How many people in distress have pondered these words!

> The Lord is my shepherd; I shall not want.
>
> He maketh me to lie down in green pastures: he leadeth me beside the still waters.
>
> He restoreth my soul: he leadeth me in the paths of righteousness for his name's sake.
>
> Yea, though I walk through the valley of the shadow of death, I will fear no evil: for thou art with me; thy rod and thy staff they comfort me.
>
> Thou preparest a table before me in the presence of mine enemies: thou anointest my head with oil; my cup runneth over.
>
> Surely goodness and mercy shall follow me all the days of my life: and I will dwell in the house of the Lord forever.

The Ultimate Freedom

My Bible companion book had given such a beautiful rendition of this Psalm by substituting for the more corporeal sense of God as Lord, the incorporeal or spiritual sense of Deity:

[Divine Love] is my shepherd; I shall not want.

[Love] maketh me to lie down in green pastures: [Love] leadeth me beside the still waters.

[Love] restoreth my soul [spiritual sense]: [Love] leadeth me in the paths of righteousness for His name's sake.

Yea, though I walk through the valley of the shadow of death, I will fear no evil: for [Love] is with me; [Love's] rod and [Love's] staff they comfort me.

[Love] prepareth a table before me in the presence of mine enemies: [Love] anointeth my head with oil; my cup runneth over.

Surely goodness and mercy shall follow me all the days of my life; and I will dwell in the house [the consciousness] of [Love] for ever.

Captured!

Over a hundred years ago, Mary Baker Eddy, the God-inspired woman who discovered the Science behind the healing method used by Jesus (which she named Christian Science), had written this spiritual rendering of the 23rd Psalm on page 578 of her book, *Science and Health with Key to the Scriptures.* She, like St. John, must have clearly felt that consciousness of Love, and now in some measure I was beginning to experience this too in spite of a constant gnawing feeling that I was unworthy of God's goodness and grace. But isn't this the amazing grace so joyously sung about? To my rescue, in my trial, came also the healing thought — the recalling of this statement by Mrs. Eddy, "Remember, thou canst be brought into no condition, be it ever so severe, where Love has not been before thee and where its tender lesson is not awaiting thee. Therefore despair not nor murmur, for that which seeketh to save, to heal, and to deliver, will guide thee, if thou seekest this guidance" (*Miscellany,* p.149).

More and more I began to see how thought dedicated to God, good, gives that wonderful sense of being protected by a power higher and

The Ultimate Freedom

greater than any human power on earth. On the cross Jesus revealed and proved this power to be divine Love with which he overcame the hatred of his enemies. It raised him from the grave to give us the assurance of eternal life. *Science and Health*, my Bible companion book, which I had carried with me during the first months of war had explained this all so beautifully. When I was captured, this book was left between other books in the house which had been my hiding place. Little did I know that it also had been found and that it would play a role in my safekeeping.

To keep my spirits up, I sang hymns. One which I remembered very well was actually a poem by the author of the Christian Science textbook. It's in her *Miscellaneous Writings* and begins with,

> O gentle presence, peace and joy and power;
> O Life divine, that owns each waiting hour,
> Thou Love that guards the nestling's faltering flight!
> Keep Thou my child on upward wing to-night.
> (p.389)

These words never failed to bring peace of mind to me. The certainty that God would provide a

Captured!

way out increased daily. I even began to see things from a detached point of view.

Now, all during this time I slept well except for one night. This particular night I was awakened with the feeling that my mentality was being tampered with, that something or someone was exercising an influence on my consciousness. (I had not been long enough in the Orient to become knowledgeable about the common practice of mental manipulation.) Yes, something was taking place that was a definite mental intrusion. I instinctively felt that I must stay awake and spiritually defend myself. This I did through prayer, through filling my consciousness with thoughts from God. After some time, the feeling suddenly ceased as if a faucet had been turned off. I forgot all about this incident until three years later when, towards the end of the war, this mysterious happening would be cleared up. (I will refer to this later.)

As days and weeks went by, my awareness of man's indestructible, immortal life in God became clearer and clearer. Passages from the Scriptures became illumined in my thought, in particular the chapter in the book of Revelation where St. John says of the holy city that "...there shall be no more death, neither sorrow, nor crying, neither shall there be any more pain:..." (Rev.21:4).

Then one day came a glimpse of what I took as a sign that God was also working in the thoughts and lives of my captors. Again taken from my cell to be questioned, we passed this time through a room where I saw a Japanese man translating from a book. Papers with Japanese writing were scattered around, and, as we passed at very close range, I saw that the book this man was copying from was my Bible companion book — *Science and Health*. There was no doubt about it! Here was my book, with its well-thumbed pages that I knew so well. A feeling of confidence and assurance came over me. I now no longer thought of myself as surrounded by enemies, but I began to see all, in reality, as under the control of God. At another time, I again saw this man working at the translation of my book.

Finally the day came when, at the end of a period of questioning conducted by the Japanese

Captured!

officer who seemed to be in charge of the prison, I was asked, through a Japanese woman interpreter, "How do you feel about dying now?" I had become so inspired and uplifted through these months of prayer and the control of my thought that the words of my answer seemed to be spoken for me: "You could not possibly kill me, for God, Spirit, created me spiritually; all you could do would be to do away with a dream about me. And if I were in your place, and you in mine, I could not kill you either; for the same God who created me spiritually, created you spiritually, and all I could do would be to do away with a dream about you." Then came the last question: "Have you any wish?" Again, as if the words were spoken for me, I answered, "Yes, I have. I wish to understand all about Life." I was then returned to my cell.

Some time later my cell door opened slightly, and the woman interpreter said softly, "Everything is going to be all right." Although my heart now sang with gratitude, my trials were not yet over. Soon a Japanese man opened the door, handed me a banana, and in a voice which

The Ultimate Freedom

indicated that something was to take place, confided, "Eat it slowly." Then followed a week during which my door remained shut and locked, and I was left without food or water, except for one night when someone thrust the spout of a kettle through the bars of my window and poured out water, which I drank.

After this week of fasting, the officer-in-charge who previously had interrogated and threatened me, now came in carrying a tray with dishes of food. During the interrogations he had spoken only in Japanese through the interpreter. Now in flawless English he said, "I have prepared this myself. Eat it slowly and you will be all right." The fact that he was dressed in a kimono this time seemed evidence to me of his good will. He bowed courteously and went on to say that I would be taken care of, and then offered to have a doctor come and examine me. I was able to say, with all truthfulness and assurance, that I was perfectly all right, that there had been no ill effects of the fasting.

The fasting had been not only a physical but also a mental and spiritual activity.

True Thinking

Controlling my thought, listening for thoughts coming from God, had not only saved my life but had enabled me to keep well physically.

Shortly after the officer in charge of the prison camp had visited me and given me food, others came and showed concern for me. My watch was returned, and I was given clothes and blankets and then taken by car to a regular prison camp. For the next three years I remained a prisoner of war, living in various prison camps on the island of Java.

Mary Baker Eddy points out that "Good thoughts are an impervious armor; clad therewith you are completely shielded from the attacks of error of every sort" (*Miscellany,* p.210). This truly had been my experience!

Dear reader, from the above statement, which I proved, that good thoughts are an armor to shield us from evil happenings, it would seem that the urgent question to be answered by each

The Ultimate Freedom

one of us is: "Do we think, or just think we think?" You will agree, I am sure, that we all seek to know the truth about things. And as this is so, we're also interested to know if our thinking is true.

Today the notion of thinking pervades our society. Research organizations are sometimes referred to as "think factories" or "think tanks". In our daily lives, we're constantly urged to think in some particular manner. Furnishing manufacturers plead, "Think color!" Beauty experts cry, "Think young!" Physical fitness promoters shout, "Think thin!" More significant is the fact that men and women of great stature have earnestly considered the question of thinking. We're probably all familiar with Shakespeare's statement, "There is nothing either good or bad, but thinking makes it so." In the Bible are these words attributed to Solomon, "...as he (a man) thinketh in his heart, so is he:..." (Prov. 23:7). And in the preface to *Science and Health with Key to the Scriptures,* Mary Baker Eddy has this rousing statement: "The time for thinkers has come" (vii).

True Thinking

Isn't it true that all of us are engaged in the business of thinking? But can we rightly say that what we call <u>thinking</u> is always true or original thinking? Isn't much of our so-called thinking just reacting to impressions or suggestions, making assumptions, or merely mulling over problems and difficulties? Many centuries ago, the Roman Emperor-Philosopher Marcus Aurelius, said: "The happiness of your life depends upon the quality of your thoughts...therefore guard them accordingly." This statement is just as true today as it was then. So the question of thinking is of vital importance to us all.

Through careful choice of the thoughts which come to us, we can do much to improve our whole life experience as well as that of our neighbors. In order to experience good more fully, we need to differentiate clearly between real thinking and what is really <u>not</u> thinking at all. Then we need to control thought — to bar the false thinking — and to keep busy with true thinking. The Bible clearly tells us what true thinking really is. The Apostle Paul wrote:

The Ultimate Freedom

...whatsoever things are true,
whatsoever things are honest,
whatsoever things are just, whatsoever
things are pure, whatsoever things are
lovely, whatsoever things are of good
report; if there be any virtue, and if
there be any praise, think on these
things.

(Phil. 4:8)

If to think on these is true thinking, then to
contemplate the opposite of what Paul lists here
— that is, falsehood, dishonesty, injustice, impurity,
unloveliness — is false thinking, or just thinking
that we are thinking when in fact we're not
thinking at all.

From the depth of his spiritual insight,
Christ Jesus explained the matter of true and false
thinking by means of a parable in the fourth
chapter of Mark. He told of a sower letting some
seed fall by the wayside where it was choked by
thorns. Then he explained that the seed
represented "the word of God," and the thorns
were the cares of the everyday world, the
misleading hopes raised by riches and general
greed. He stated that those listeners who "hear

the word, and receive it" will be fruitful, or as we might say, will do useful, effective thinking and experience the good results of that thinking.

As a boy of twelve, Jesus was able to talk with the learned men in the temple and later men marvelled how he came to have so much wisdom and learning. Jesus always ascribed all power to God, even his ability to think; for he said, "...whatsoever I speak therefore, even as the Father said unto me, so I speak" (John 12:50). Obviously he equated true thinking with listening to the word of God, and failure to think with listening to the suggestions of evil. Jesus rejected any suggestion of evil that came to him with such rebukes as, "Get thee behind me, Satan."

His whole life was a prayer, a prayer of listening. Jesus always listened to the Father. And he told others, "...and the word which ye hear is not mine, but the Father's which sent me" (John 14:24). Many of the outstanding men and women in the Bible had extraordinary ability to listen for thoughts coming from God. In the Old Testament, men like Jacob, Moses, and Jeremiah heard such messages. They described these

The Ultimate Freedom

communications in statements such as, "Then the word of the Lord came to me, saying,..." (Jer.18:5) or simply as, "And God said,..." (Gen.9:12). These men heard God's thoughts when they prayed. Their receptivity then resulted in clear direction for human action as when Moses was inspired to go to the Pharaoh and demand the release of the children of Israel who were held in bondage.

In the New Testament (Luke 1:35) we read of Mary, the mother-to-be of Jesus, conversing with an angel who said to her, "The Holy Ghost shall come upon thee, and the power of the Highest shall overshadow thee: therefore also that holy thing which shall be born of thee shall be called the Son of God." Angels, according to the definition given in *Science and Health,* are "God's thoughts passing to man; spiritual intuitions, pure and perfect;..." (p.581). Matthew writes that the angel of the Lord appeared unto Joseph in a dream, saying, "Joseph, thou son of David, fear not to take unto thee Mary thy wife: for that which is conceived in her is of the Holy Ghost. And she shall bring forth a son, and thou shalt call his name JESUS:..." (Matt. 1:20,21).

True Thinking

The Bible gives us abundant proof that men can listen to God speak and can receive perfect instructions to live by. This was the practical lesson I learned during my time of trial — that, shutting out worldly thoughts, doubts, and fears, we can listen for God's directions and receive divine guidance. Shakespeare spoke truly when he said,

> Sweet are the uses of adversity;
> Which, like the toad, ugly and venomous,
> Wears yet a precious jewel in his head.

And so did the discoverer of Christian Science speak truly when she said, "The very circumstance, which your suffering sense deems wrathful and afflictive, Love can make an angel entertained unawares" (*Science and Health*, p.574).

The Ultimate Freedom

As this book is not intended to be a record of the cruelties of war, but rather to show that some understanding of true thinking brings peace and a sense of protection and guidance, I will deal only with a few incidents to illustrate this.

Most of these years of imprisonment were spent working on a piece of land about an hour's march away from the camp. I had volunteered to act as overseer of a group of soldiers charged with the task of converting barren soil into a vegetable farm to provide vegetables (a vinelike plant) for our prison diet. Prior to my offer, several officers had volunteered for this job, but had soon given it up because of the constant difficulties between prisoners and guards resulting in the beating of both the soldier and the overseeing officer.

During my three-month period of solitary confinement I became convinced that all men are truly under God's direction. And this conviction finally gained for me the respect and trust of both the guards and the farm commandant. The

34

prisoners, too, evidenced this respect and trust, for incidents of misunderstanding or disobedience were few.

However, one such incident did occur, a lesson as I see it now in Christlike behavior. For this was what my prisoner-of-war experience, like any other trial, was about — learning to practice Christianity. One morning while I was walking around the farm, my attention was suddenly drawn to screams coming from the direction of a road which led along the barbed wire fence.

Hurrying to where the screams issued from, I came upon an ugly scene. Here was a prisoner writhing on the ground while a stockily-built guard rained blows on him with the butt of his rifle. The prisoner was obviously in very bad shape, and the sight of this made me impulsively push the enraged guard away. I then kneeled to comfort the prisoner and to inquire what had taken place. Bit by bit it came out. He had climbed a tree, to which the barbed wire fence was attached, to cut some of the branches for firewood. And this had enraged the guard, a Korean, who probably thought he was trying to escape.

The Ultimate Freedom

From the corner of my eye, I could see this guard hurrying toward the guardhouse only to return with two more guards. To my astonishment, these new arrivals, on seeing the hurt soldier and hearing my vehement protestations of the man's innocence, took hold of the enraged Korean and led him away. With the help of another prisoner, the hurt soldier was then carried to a shelter, and he remained there for the rest of the day. This, however, was not to be the end of the incident.

When time came to line up the prisoners to be counted preparatory to marching back to the camp, the Korean who had done the beating appeared again carrying a 4 by 4 post. I had gone to the injured soldier and put his arm around my neck to help him to a small tool cart used to carry shovels and other equipment, when this guard came toward us with the post raised above his head. To forsake the incapacitated soldier would have been unthinkable. He could barely drag himself along, and so I kept on walking with him right toward the infuriated guard. To make matters worse, the prisoners now began to shout and curse, and I feared a riot.

When only a few feet away from us, the Korean suddenly dropped the post and disappeared behind the commandant's hut. At that moment I reached the tool cart and laid the hurt man on it. Then, from the group of other guards who had been watching the scene, two guards approached and ordered me to take two more prisoners to help push the cart so we could hurry to the camp while they accompanied us.

Looking back several times on the way, I could see the column of prisoners following in the distance. The injured man was carried into the camp to receive aid, and this closed the incident. The guard who had done the beating did not appear the next morning and never again accompanied us to the farm. The overcoming of fear truly does go hand-in-hand with spiritual growth, and as in this case, the reward was such a blessing. From that time, the Japanese farm commandant and his guards seemed to have more trust in me, while my trust in good had grown stronger.

The Ultimate Freedom

Fortunately, prisoner-of-war life was not all grimness. There were lighter moments, too. One prisoner, called Norman, and I had become good friends. He was a cultured man with several degrees who, in private life, held a high position in government. We usually ate our evening meal of rice, sprinkled with some leaves and at times fish powder, together. During these times we would have some stimulating discussions, Norman being well versed in Oriental and European philosophy.

Besides being a wise and kindly man, he was an imposing figure as he strode through the camp, smoking a homemade cigar, dressed only in a pair of khaki trousers strung up half mast and patched in numerous places with the usual green patches obtained from worn-out Dutch uniforms. Besides a very dilapidated pair of old shoes, turned up at the toes, he also wore around his neck a black ribbon from which dangled a monocle. His old-world courtesy shone like a precious stone among the prisoners and even the

A Humorous Incident

Japanese, whose processes of thought he seemed to understand thoroughly, treated him with some deference. Being an architect among other things, he was often called upon by them to solve building and other problems.

Now the prisoners slept in long bamboo barracks on bamboo stretchers running the full length of the huts, each with his own clamboo (mosquito net) supplied by the Japanese. There were about fifty to sixty men in a barrack. Norman's place was next to me and he was a heavy snorer. This kept me and others awake particularly when, in the middle of the night, he would at intervals let out especially loud eerie sounding noises. Then there would be groans and curses from the other men but Norman would sleep on... and keep on snoring! Having to rise between four and five in the morning to march to the farm and feeling I needed my sleep, I finally began to defend myself against this snoring by banging on the bamboo trestle with my fist, and then there would be silence for awhile.

One afternoon after returning to the camp from the farm, I found Norman in a very serious mood. He said he had been thinking about something but just did not quite know how to broach it to me. He felt it would be best to make an appointment with me for some days ahead. In the meantime he would consider how best to reveal this serious situation. My assurances that no matter what it was, it would be fine to tell me there and then, did not move him from his determination to make a proper appointment at a given hour. I agreed to this, and for the next few days puzzled as to what might be weighing so heavily on my friend's mind. What could possibly cause him to be so formal and downright mysterious?

At the agreed hour we sat down and Norman began with many comforting statements that what he was about to say was for my own good, and that he was only going to speak to me because of our friendship and his concern for my well-being. After much uhming, aahing and prompting he finally came out with it. He had, it appeared, been greatly concerned about my mental health, and his advice to me as his friend was that I see a psychiatrist as soon as we were freed. He confided that he had noticed very troubling signs which led him to believe all was not well with me mentally and emotionally.

He said that nearly every night I had, in my sleep, banged violently on the bamboo trestle, waking him up. He had, at length, come to the conclusion that I must be in the grip of some dire mental disturbance caused through our long period of imprisonment. He was very sorry to have to tell me this he said apologetically, but after weighing the matter carefully, had felt duty-bound to reveal his finding to me in order that I might be cured of my trouble.

Well, I never told Norman what really had been going on, but the incident gave me many a good chuckle, which I really needed at that time.

MENTAL INFLUENCES

Now only once during these years was there an occasion when I received a blow, but even that was a valuable lesson — never to let anything or anyone persuade you to act against your better judgment.

One particularly strong-willed soldier kept insisting that he should be made assistant overseer. I felt his insistence mentally as well as verbally. Finally I yielded to the mental pressure which seemed to deprive me of my right thinking, and so the man put down his shovel and began walking around acting as overseer. Within minutes, a guard spotted him and gave him a beating. He was then brought over to me protesting that I had told him to do what he did; and that is when I received a severe blow in the face.

How often do we suffer painful consequences through yielding to false influence! To recognize these thought-pressures as erring human will either in ourselves or in others and rejecting them as contrary to the will of God, good, is our protection in such cases. After this incident, I was more determined to watch that my thinking was not broken into by either audible or inaudible suggestions.

Mental Influences

I learned too that people in the Orient appear in many ways to have developed a keen sense for discerning insincerity and dishonesty as well as danger. The following incident illustrates this point. As I mentioned, the prisoners had to dig hard dry earth and do this under a scorching tropical sun. Their thoughts ranged from dull despair to violent revenge. On this particular day one of the guards, a rather quiet, kindly Korean, who usually walked around unarmed among the prisoners, ordered me to come with him to interpret something he wanted to tell a prisoner. On reaching the prisoner, who worked away from the others in a secluded spot, I was told to tell him that if he persisted in his bad thoughts, he would be severely punished. The guard then walked away.

Filled with curiosity, I inquired of my fellow-prisoner the meaning of all this. He admitted he had often thought that, if one of those guards would ever come near and be alone with him he would bash the guard's head in with his shovel. So violent was the suggestion of hatred and vengefulness which he had accepted

The Ultimate Freedom

into his consciousness that the guard had sensed the thoughts and intentions of the prisoner. If the guard had been a less kindly man the prisoner's thoughts might have landed him in severe punishment. *Science and Health* tells us, "You must control evil thoughts in the first instance, or they will control you in the second" (p.234). Evil thoughts such as those accepted by my fellow-prisoner — thoughts which may have resulted in the killing of a man — are in the Bible referred to by Paul as the carnal mind, when he says in Romans (8:6,7) "To be carnally minded is death; but to be spiritually minded is life and peace. Because the carnal mind is enmity against God: for it is not subject to the law of God, neither indeed can be."

Isn't right thinking then a question of being spiritually minded which the Bible says is life and peace, and keeping out such thoughts as revenge, hatred, malice, etc? Doesn't the Bible urge us to, "Let this mind be in you, which was also in Christ Jesus" (Phil. 2:5). Jesus is the best example. His consciousness was filled with thoughts from God. Christian Science clears up any misunderstanding

Mental Influences

concerning Jesus the Christ (as he was named in the Greek) and gives the proper understanding of Christ Jesus in these revealing statements found in *Science and Health* (p. 332):

> Jesus was born of Mary. Christ is the true idea voicing good, the divine message from God to men speaking to the human consciousness... As Paul says: 'There is one God, and one mediator between God and men, the man Christ Jesus.' The corporeal man Jesus was human.

The Christ, then, is not a human person but the divine image or true idea of God, which Jesus so completely represented. The Christ is present and available to heal and save at all times and in all places. It is the Christ which enables us to listen to God and receive divine guidance.

Chapter Two

CHRISTMAS IN CAMP

We can expect to hear what the Christ has to say to us, and we can expect others, regardless of race, color or creed, to also hear the divine message.

I experienced an instance of this when, as time passed, the morale and health of many of the prisoners in our camp became steadily worse. Food was insufficient, and the things which were considered necessary to a proper diet were not available. That year just before Christmas, I was asked by the camp doctor, also a prisoner of war, if I would try to persuade the Japanese farm commandant to purchase a supply of fruit from the nearby villages. He said this might help save the lives of some prisoners who were suffering from beri-beri and other diseases.

The Ultimate Freedom

Money had been collected for this purpose, and I was given a small roll of bills to pay for the fruit should I be successful in my request. Praying as to how I might approach this matter, I made my way to the commandant's hut. His expression, as I stood there before his desk, conveyed that I would never get through to him. Then the thought came to me, "Tell him about Christmas." This was a startling thought to me at the time as I considered this Japanese man, apparently a Shintoist, to have no idea of either Christ or Christmas. Overcoming my reluctance, I obeyed my intuition and proceeded in a mixture of languages to convey, as best I could, the meaning of Christmas as I understood it in Christian Science. I spoke of the Christ idea, of men's true brotherhood, of love and goodwill toward each other. Then I asked to have much fruit brought from the villages so that Christmas might have a real meaning for those men sick in the camp.

All this time I was met with stony silence. There seemed not a flicker of comprehension nor sympathy. As a last attempt, I repeated some of the thoughts I had tried to convey and placed the roll of money on the desk. The money was swept brusquely aside. I left with not a single clue as to what had been understood of my plea. Still I refused to feel disappointment or resentment. I knew that I and all men, both captives and captors, in reality lived, moved and had their being in a spiritual dimension, in a God-controlled realm.

Some days later when making the rounds of the field, I saw a very excited guard on a bicycle riding towards me, gesturing and shouting to me to come at once. He began pushing me in the back to make me run, shouting in French, "Courez, courez!" ("Run, run!") My first thought was that somewhere another beating was taking place and that my presence was required. However, I was rushed to the commandant's hut and told to go inside. There behind his desk was the commandant, a broad grin on his face, and on the floor around him several Javanese squatting beside huge baskets full of fruit. Astonished and grateful, I stepped forward and put the roll of money I was still carrying with me on the desk. Again it was brusquely swept aside, but this time,

The Ultimate Freedom

I could hardly believe my eyes and ears. Pointing at his chest, the commandant repeated, "Kismis, Kismis," and with that he took money out of his own pocket and paid for the fruit.

I can tell you that that day the men made a joyful entrance into the camp pushing a cart loaded with the fruit. The Christ-spirit was really felt that Christmas. Even the guards seemed to take part in the excitement. Yes, the Christ-spirit had broken through the barriers of race, hate, and despair. All men truly have one God and Father. It is the Christ which bridges the gap men have placed between themselves and God. Through the Christ-message received by me and understood also by the Japanese commandant, a so-called enemy had actually proved himself to be a generous friend on that occasion.

UNIVERSAL BROTHERHOOD

Yes, the action of the Christ, when it is entertained in consciousness, fulfills Jesus' commandment, "That ye love one another, as I

Universal Brotherhood

have loved you" (John 15:12). Such a Christian ideal transcends religious beliefs and finds a response in the hearts of men everywhere. Mary Baker Eddy writes, "Jesus demonstrated Christ; he proved that Christ is the divine idea of God — the Holy Ghost, or Comforter, revealing the divine Principle, Love, and leading into all truth" (*Science and Health*, p.332).

We also demonstrate this Christ when our thoughts, and consequently our actions, are pure — when they are in harmony with God, Truth, and so solve our human relationship problems. Yes, racial strife and hatred are doomed to be extinguished, for the Christ knocks at the door of humanity insisting on its universal acceptance. Through a scientific understanding of the Christ, men will find a new way for living together in universal brotherhood, seeing each other as they really are, God's spiritual ideas, the beloved of Love. Isn't the world today really crying out for a whole new dimension for living, one that is free from hate, fear, and the host of other evils that plague mankind? And isn't this to be achieved through a revolution in individual thinking routing the enemies of fear, ignorance and sin?

Over the ages, human efforts to bring peace to mankind have proved inadequate. Spiritualization of thought is mankind's only path to peace. As Paul states it, "The fruit of the Spirit is love, joy, peace, longsuffering, gentleness, goodness, faith, meekness, temperance: against such there is no law" (Gal. 5:22,23). Indeed no laws of punishment would be required if men entertained this Spirit in their thoughts and hearts.

You can see, dear reader, that with even the small understanding gained through obeying as best I could the command to control the thoughts that came to me, rejecting base and evil thoughts and listening for guidance and direction from above, my prisoner-of-war experience had become an adventure rather than a nightmare. And although, because of lack of food, I had become a shadow of my former self, yet during those entire three years in the camp I experienced no sickness at all.

There was something else that happened during my imprisonment that also proves that the

Universal Brotherhood

Christ does influence human consciousness. (This is the incident referred to earlier when I said that my Bible companion book would play a part in my safekeeping.) From time to time a list was posted with names of prisoners who were to be sent by ship to prisoner-of-war camps in Japan. The idea of being held captive in Japan was hardly appealing, but there was an additional danger to this. The ships were so often torpedoed by the Allies that prisoners were considered fortunate to make it to Japan at all.

My name would suddenly disappear from these lists. And though twice I was paraded with other prisoners in the middle of the night for this purpose, both times I was singled out and sent back to the barracks. It was not until the end of the war when I met the man who had worked on the translation of *Science and Health* that this mystery was explained. In fluent English, he said he was a member of the Japanese secret police, had become a student of the book and that he had kept me safe. Here again, through the influence of the Christ an enemy had become a friend, though I was totally unaware of this at the time.

The Ultimate Freedom

There were not only moments of joy and mirth during these trying years, but also moments of touching beauty and even grandeur when the human spirit would rise to unexpected heights transcending the ugliness of hate and fear. One such time was on the 25th of April, celebrated as ANZAC Day (Australian and New Zealand Army Corps).

The work party, marching each day to Tanjong Oost, was mostly made up of what were rugged Australian soldiers, many of whom had come from the Australian outback and who were used to a tough life. The nearly three years of hardship and deprivation they had by this time endured, however, had reduced them to a ragged bunch of mostly dispirited men, desperately hanging onto the hope that one day their comrades would come and deliver them.

This particular day their spirits were at an all-time low as they reminisced among themselves about the days gone by when, in their homeland,

ANZAC Day

ANZAC Day meant remembering past glory on the battlefields of Europe during the First World War. In the morning there would be colorful parades with stirring marches and solemn ceremonies everywhere. At 11 o'clock people would gather in town and city squares around monuments honoring the fallen. At this hour, with everyone standing at attention, a bugler would sound the "Last Post," followed by one minute of silence.

Now that morning on the Tanjong Oost farm was a particularly beautiful one. The air was still and an almost unearthly feeling pervaded the atmosphere. My heart went out to those men, and I began to cast about in my thought if there were not something that could be done to break the spell of gloom and give them a renewed sense of dignity and worth. Then an idea presented itself — one that at first seemed not only foolhardy but highly dangerous. Then again, I reasoned the situation was already highly dangerous with men succumbing to despondence, illness, and some even to the lack of will to live. We had a bugler with us who would blow his bugle each morning

The Ultimate Freedom

for reveille and then again for rest breaks, lunch, and falling in to go back to the camp in the evening.

How would it be, I reasoned, if the Japanese commandant would grant permission to have this man sound the "Last Post" at the stroke of eleven, and allow the men to stand to attention for sixty seconds. The idea seemed unthinkable at first, because no concerted action of any kind was allowed. The rules laid down by the Japanese Command were most specific on this issue.

As I said before, I had begun to rely heavily on intuition, and I now felt a compelling urge to attempt to carry out this plan. I walked around the field and spoke with a number of the men, also with the bugler. All said it would be something to really raise their spirits. ANZAC Day on Tanjong Oost! What a fantastic possibility! Next I went to the commandant's hut, where I found him sitting at his desk. One thing that helped me to believe that this man would listen to my proposal was the fact that over the past months I noticed he had begun to trust me even further. For instance, the guards were no longer constantly patrolling the farm but remained in the watchtowers spaced around the perimeter of the camp. In a mixture of Malay and English I conveyed my plan, holding firmly to the thought that all men are brethren under God and not hateful enemies. The Japanese commandant listened patiently as I repeated my request several times. Not a word was said by him, but that in itself I had learned was not a bad sign.

I then went back to the men and told them I had put the plan to the commandant and if they agreed I would inform the bugler. They had talked among themselves and did agree. The lack of hate and fear I had felt in myself ever since my experience in the Bandung jail and my desire to live the life that would express the highest type of Christianity had given me the strong assurance that God is supreme and that Christianity is not just a form of religion but the right way of living and acting.

With 11 o'clock approaching, I realized that the guards in the towers did not know anything of what was to happen. How would they react when the bugle was blown at an unusual time and all the men would drop their shovels and stand to attention?

Then just minutes before 11 o'clock, a guard on a bicycle came from the direction of the commandant's hut and rode at full speed from one watch tower to the other shouting what I sensed were instructions. A devilish thought presented itself to me. He's telling them to shoot! I dismissed this thought in the manner I had learned previously and replaced it with the one that these men were only capable of expressing love and kindness. Christlike qualities they, too, had inherited from their heavenly Father.

Never had the "Last Post" sounded as it did in the stillness and clarity of that morning. It was a most touching experience as if a beautiful prayer were being prayed. All the some hundred or more prisoners stood to attention for what seemed the longest minute. Then looking in the direction of the guard towers, I saw the most astonishing and inspiring sight. Every guard stood to attention with us. The one who had gone around had laid his bicycle on the ground and also stood there stiffly to attention. During that one minute

ANZAC Day

legions of angels ministered to us I felt. I had
seen Christianity in action as I had not seen it
before, not on such a scale. The spirit of Christ
had surely defeated the powers of evil. That
evening the men marched with vigor in their step,
heads held high. That ANZAC Day became
something very precious for us all.

Chapter Three

A NATION'S STRUGGLE

Towards the end of the war, we were transferred to a camp in Batavia, now called Jakarta, to work in what appeared to have been a car assembly plant. It was there that I met the man who would clear up the mystery of the experience I had in the jail when I was awakened in the middle of the night with the feeling that my mentality was being tampered with. This man, dressed in civilian clothes, was brought, with others, into the compound. He was a Javanese who told me, when I spoke with him one day, that he remembered me well although I did not recollect ever having seen him. He said he had been employed at the prison where I had been kept in solitary confinement.

It seems he had been present the night when my captors had attempted to subject me to mental manipulation, or suggestion, for the purpose of questioning me. The reason he remembered me so well, he said, was that this attempt to manipulate me mentally had no effect on me whatever. He was so impressed by this that he had noted my name, rank and service number. Now whether he was the actual man employed to do this, I did not find out, but that such mental manipulation is the very opposite of receiving inspiration from God should be understood by us all and guarded against. It is necessary, therefore, to give much thought to thought and to ask ourselves, "Do you think or just think you think?" The answer to this all-important question lies in these words of Jesus, our Way-shower, "I can of mine own self do nothing: as I hear, I judge; and my judgment is just; because I seek not mine own will, but the will of the Father which hath sent me" (John 5:30).

We live in a thought world and are constantly confronted with having to make choices between fallible human concepts (sometimes in the form of aggressive mental suggestions) and spiritual ideas. What enables us to make the right choice at all times is spiritual understanding. Christian Science teaches, "Understanding is the line of demarcation between the real and unreal" (*Science and Health,* p.505). This spiritual understanding is inherent in all of us and can be developed. I found it through study of the Bible together with the book, *Science and Health.* Without this spiritual understanding we are more or less like a rudderless ship tossed to and fro by prevailing mental winds and waves. With it, we can steer a straight course and meet every obstacle with a sense of adventure, knowing it to be an opportunity for higher achievement.

The work in the car assembly plant was of short duration. There were rumors flying around that the Japanese had put us there so that if the Allies bombed the plant we would be targets and this then could be a propaganda weapon. In a short time, however, we were no longer required to work in the plant and were kept in the confines of an erstwhile Dutch military camp in the center of Batavia.

This Batavia camp was now beginning to be so packed with prisoners that it seemed obvious something extraordinary was afoot. Suddenly I was sent for — to appear at the guard house. I was told I was to be taken to Bandung for questioning. Now, over three years had passed since my interrogations in the Bandung jail, and I could not imagine what this might be about. Under heavy guard I was taken to the railway station and then by train to the city where my war experience had commenced. This time the jail I was lodged in consisted of a string of cages facing a small courtyard. These cages were filled with civilians, some with men, others with women. I was put in the end cage, alone.

Several days went by during which time I was allowed once or twice, with others, to walk in the courtyard and do some exercises, but always with a guard. Then one morning I was taken to a room for questioning. It concerned my diary. When I was captured, I had just found time to push this diary through a ceiling opening in one of the small rooms of the pavilion before attempting to escape over the back wall. Evidently a thorough search had been made and the diary had been found. In it, as I mentioned before, I had

A Nation's Struggle

written some observations and philosophical considerations on the drama I had become involved in — predicting the war would be lost by the Japanese, and the resulting effect on the Indonesians.

Having arrived in Java before the war with Japan, I had seen the effects of colonization on the Indonesian people. Their state was almost that of slavery where servants were made to work endless hours for as little as ten Dutch cents per day. I had written in this diary how I foresaw the end of the three hundred and fifty years of Dutch colonization through the present war. I had also written down how I thought the Indonesians might enlist the help of those who, I felt sure, would one day come to liberate Java from its present invaders.

The idea had presented itself to me in this way: There would surely be mostly Americans who would come to free us. Having lived some three years in the United States, I had become familiar with their early history and with those marvelous documents — "The Declaration of Independence" and "The Constitution of the

The Ultimate Freedom

United States of America." I had learned in school in Holland that among the early settlers of America there had been Dutch as well as English whose main reason for leaving their homeland had been religious freedom. Freedom, I knew, was considered by Americans as the basic right of everyone. I felt God would surely help the Indonesians to attain theirs through what was now happening.

The sentence, from "The Declaration of Independence," which stood out most to me begins with, "We hold these truths to be self-evident, that all men are created equal,..." I had written in my diary that this sentence should be painted by the Indonesians in large letters on the many stone walls in the city of Batavia where the American liberators would surely see the words.

The interrogation I was now subjected to centered around the Japanese's suspicion that, before I was captured, I had been in touch with Javanese political groups striving for freedom from Dutch rule — and, of course, I hadn't. Then a young Javanese man, dressed in Western clothes — perhaps one who had belonged to some such group — was brought in, and again I was pressed to tell why I had written such a statement and who I had known, and did I know him. I protested that my only reason for writing what I did was because of my firm belief that all men should be free and that God, I felt sure, was providing a way for the people of Indonesia to gain their freedom.

I was finally returned to my cell, and the next day I was taken by train back to the prisoner-of-war camp in Batavia. The speculation as to what was happening in the theater of war became more intense daily, but the Japanese gave no indication that things had gone against them. They carried on their routine roll calls and inspections as usual. Then one morning we woke up to a day the prisoners of war of the Japanese will never forget. The Japanese had surrendered. Atom bombs had brought the war to an abrupt end, and now the tables were turned. This brought about a great deal of activity. Planes came over and dropped supplies, and preparations for the evacuation of prisoners were set in motion.

The Ultimate Freedom

It was while being taken to a new location in Batavia that I had a most surprising experience. Along the way we passed a high stone wall on which was painted in very large white letters, in English, "We hold these truths to be self-evident, that all men are created equal, that they are endowed by their Creator with certain unalienable rights, that among these are Life, Liberty and the pursuit of Happiness." It is a matter of history that the Javanese people obtained this precious human freedom and that the Dutch found that their prosperity did not depend on the labor and efforts of an enslaved people.

Mary Baker Eddy , taking the meaning of liberty to its highest sense, writes in *Science and Health* (p.227):

> Discerning the rights of man, we cannot fail to foresee the doom of all oppression. Slavery is not the legitimate state of man. God made man free. Paul said, 'I was free born.' All men should be free. 'Where the Spirit of the Lord is, there is liberty.' Love and Truth make free, but evil and error lead into captivity.

68

A Nation's Struggle

Christian Science raises the standard of liberty and cries: 'Follow me! Escape from the bondage of sickness, sin, and death!' Jesus marked out the way. Citizens of the world, accept the 'glorious liberty of the children of God,' and be free! This is your divine right.

Part II

Breaking Out of Captivity in Freedom

Part II

Breaking Out of Captivity in Freedom

Chapter Four

THE EMPLOYMENT QUESTION

The war ended with the surrender of the Japanese to the American and Allied forces, and those of us who had survived the prison camps in the Orient were flown or shipped back to our respective countries.

Reunited with my family in Australia, I was now faced with rehabilitation to normal civilian life. My immediate concern was to find some meaningful work to provide for myself, wife, son and daughter. This at first did not appear so simple mainly because of my changed mental outlook. The idea of engaging in something just to make money seemed repulsive to me now. I had seen God work in my affairs in such wonderful ways and I wanted this way of life to continue. I had been declared by the military authorities to be in perfect health and was told that if I should like to take a course of some sort at a school or university I would be paid a small living allowance. I had no desire to return to the work I had been doing prior to the war and I waited for some new idea to come to me.

Gradually it dawned on me what I should like to do. It came simply in this way: As I listened for guidance, ideas unfolded. The first thought was: "You will be happy only if you satisfy your inner craving for beauty." This craving for beauty had taken the form of filling our small apartment with the most beautiful flowers I could find, replacing them every few days so as not to have one single blighted leaf or bud. Our apartment adjoined a garden belonging to a hospital. I called on the matron-in-charge and received permission to take out every other paling of a wooden fence which had blocked our view. Now our home was filled with sunlight and looked out on a scene of the most glorious flowering trees and shrubs.

I installed wall lamps, laid new floorings, and transformed a rather austere dwelling into a place of beauty. I just could not stop beautifying. It was like feeling a great hunger that couldn't be satisfied. The reason I am telling you this is that this urge to beautify my surroundings was to have an important bearing on my future business career and prosperity. It appears to be a law that if we improve what we have to the utmost, we inevitably rise to higher achievements.

The second thought that unfolded to me as I kept on listening was: "Whatever you do must bless others and beautify their lives." Then came the third and final one: "You must do the thing you love to do most to be really successful." I now had a basis from which to proceed and felt sure God's plan for me would be revealed.

Before being sent abroad on military duty, I had served as an instructor at an Air Force

The Ultimate Freedom

Engineering School and had used charts, slides, and films to teach airmen. Here was my answer. I would like to go into a business where all these things could be developed together, to beautify and enrich peoples' lives. But how? On making inquiries, I found that no school or college taught such courses. The term "audio-visual" was not known here.

At that time, in discussing my desire with a government official, he suggested that I could perhaps find some company to teach me what I wanted to learn and the government would still pay me the small grant. The pieces were beginning to fit together.

Then a friend of the family called on us and I told him of my desire to learn various visual and sound techniques to combine them in an expression of art and beauty. The making of educational films, I told him, would be number one on my list. This friend was the means of introducing me to a man (for confidentiality reasons, I will call him Andrew Ainsworth) who had a commercial and industrial photographic business. Ainsworth had also made some

The Employment Question

educational and promotional films and now wanted to branch out into the film field. An interview was arranged and I was given the opportunity to enter Mr. Ainsworth's business as a pupil in the film section. This section consisted of just one man who was then in the process of making a short advertising film. I became this man's eager assistant and pupil.

During the war years Mr. Ainsworth's activities had been reduced to a very small flow of business. He had been forced to move the business to an extremely unpretentious address near the waterfront where he had rented an empty upper floor of an old warehouse owned by auctioneers of secondhand goods. Now that the war was over a number of employees had come back to claim their old jobs, and my previous management experience told me that Mr. Ainsworth was having a hard time making financial ends meet.

I received the small government grant that had been promised and so found my family and I could subsist on this, plus funds from a sum of

The Ultimate Freedom

accumulated pay I had received from the Air Force.

During the next few weeks I learned much about lighting a set, reading a light meter, loading a camera and setting lens apertures. As mentioned before I was a most industrious pupil, a real eager beaver! A sense that God's guiding hand was continuing with me made my apprenticeship a real joy though it mainly entailed unreeling light cables, and the unloading, loading, carrying, and packing up of equipment. Then events took a remarkable turn.

It must have been only a matter of some months since the day I started when a letter arrived from the government asking me to have an enclosed form signed by Mr. Ainsworth. This form was to confirm that I was indeed a pupil in his business. I took the papers to his office and was told by the secretary, in the waiting room, that Mr. Ainsworth was alone and if I just knocked on his door he would surely see me. After knocking several times and getting no response, I returned to the secretary and asked what I should do. She said to open the door and peek in. I did this and

The Employment Question

was surprised to see Mr. Ainsworth stretched out on the floor apparently in great distress. Bending over him, I asked if he wished me to do something for him. He confided that he suffered from severe back trouble which the doctors had not been able to cure and which now seemed to have reached a climax.

I offered to help him home and as we drove the long way there it seemed only right to tell him how the study of my little Bible companion book, together with the Bible, had healed me and members of my family. A close relative, I related, had been healed of an internal growth. I assured him that this same healing method, practiced by Jesus and available today, would surely heal him of his spinal trouble.

The next day I went out to see him, brought *Science and Health*, and he promised to read it. During that visit Mr. Ainsworth proposed to arrange to have some of his shares in his company transferred to me if I would undertake to manage his business while he stayed home to work out his problem. (As it turned out, as a youngster he had attended a Christian Science

The Ultimate Freedom

Sunday School and had some understanding of the wonderful healing possibilities this Science offered.)

You can imagine, that from my being a pupil to suddenly being made Managing Director of the company, there was consternation and upheaval among some of the employees. The production manager left, together with a salesman and so did the film producer and Mr. Ainsworth's secretary. The rest of the employees remained calm and assured me of their full cooperation which they indeed gave. The fact that some salaried employees now had left the company relieved a very tight financial situation, and this afforded the business some stability.

Chapter Five

PAYDAY AND ETHICS

However, things were not to remain calm for long because even the photographic business, which was the financial mainstay of the company, fluctuated so badly that one payday not long after I had started to manage, I found there was not sufficient money in the bank to pay the salaries.

In the privacy of my office I prayed earnestly to quiet my fears. I remember saying to God that I could not possibly accept the responsibility for employees having to go home to their families without money for food and other necessities. So I had to throw my burden on Him while affirming my faith in His willingness and ability to care for all. I denied the suggestion that any of God's children could lack or be embarrassed. Hadn't Jesus proved this when he fed the five thousand men besides women and children with only a few loaves and fishes that were available?

About 2:30 the girl whose job it was to go to the bank came with the payroll check for me to sign. I said I would call when I was ready and then continued praying. I raised my thought into that spiritual dimension where I had learned man forever dwells as the beloved child of God. About 2:45 the girl came again. Time was short, she said, and could she have the check? Again, I had to ask her to wait. Now I really had to vehemently deny the suggestions of fear and failure and strongly claim God's presence and God's allness.

Minutes before the hour, the girl again appeared together with a messenger boy. She could just make it to the bank before the 3 o'clock closing, she said. Then the boy spoke up. His boss had sent him around with a check, which although not due, he thought I might like to have. It was an advance on work we were doing. You can imagine with what gratitude I signed the salary check and then asked the girl to deposit the other check at the same time. It was from a nationally

Payday and Ethics

known company and would be honored on sight. Again I had a proof of God's continuing ever-present love.

Mary Baker Eddy in her *Miscellaneous Writings* (p.306) gives us this assurance, which we all can prove:

> The Psalmist saith: 'He shall give His angels charge over thee.' God gives you His spiritual ideas, and in turn, they give you daily supplies. Never ask for to-morrow: it is enough that divine Love is an ever-present help; and if you wait, never doubting, you will have all you need every moment.

To illustrate further how a spiritual idea supplied my need, I would like to give you the following example. The business owed a debt to someone who had advanced money for advertising in a magazine our company hoped to publish. This, however, did not eventuate and we received a call from this man's office to please return the money at the earliest. Looking for ways to satisfy this demand, I found we had a spare 16mm film projector, an automatic slide projector and some

related equipment on which we might realize
enough money to pay the debt. Advertisements
were placed in a newspaper, but no buyer
appeared.

Then a spiritual idea came to me in the
form of a Bible passage in Luke where Jesus is
recorded saying to his disciples, "As ye would that
men should do to you, do ye also to them
likewise" (Luke 6:31). I reasoned that if I were
owed this money I would certainly like to know
that an effort was being made to discharge the
debt, and that I should love this man enough to
explain to him just what steps were being taken.
So I made an appointment with his secretary to
see him the next morning.

Opening his door to the reception room
where I was waiting to see him, he came over to
me with outstretched hand, greeted me warmly
and said, "Am I glad to see you!" A devilish little
thought whispered, "He is glad to see you because
he thinks he is going to get the money." Once
inside his office and just about to start my
explanation, I was interrupted by my friend's
saying that he was especially happy to see me

because I might be able to help him with a dilemma.

He was the manager of a large clothing manufacturing concern and had constructed a room in his factory to show training films and slides. He had tried to buy new equipment but had found that this equipment was not available and was not then being imported. He thought I might be able to help him. Imagine my delight and gratitude as he proceeded to enumerate the items he needed, which were the very things I had been trying to sell. The debt was settled then and there, and the equipment delivered the next day. This transaction was the means of our company subsequently doing a good deal of happy and profitable business with this man by making new training films and slides for him.

God's ways are indeed wonderful. Love had met both our needs. No wonder Christian Scientists have written this statement by Mary Baker Eddy on the walls of so many of their churches, "Divine Love always has met and always will meet every human need" (*Science and Health,* p.494).

The Ultimate Freedom

Then an interesting challenge presented itself. At my request the accountant, who would come periodically to do the bookkeeping, gave me an overall view of the financial state of the company and a list of the clients we could depend on to give us regular business. These accounts were very few indeed and the major one among these few was a whiskey advertising account. This company had supplied regular business all during the war and had provided a steady income to the company.

Here was the challenge. Was I going to trust God to supply the business we so sorely needed at that moment, or was I going to trust the sale of whiskey? In my heart I knew the answer, but it seemed only right to consult with Mr. Ainsworth who was the main shareholder in our company. He said he would trust my decision and so the whiskey account was duly cancelled. Immediately new business started to flow in and the previous income from the whiskey account was more than compensated for.

Beauty and Business

With enough business coming in now to meet our present needs and with me doing the work of the production manager, my thought turned to the company surroundings. The premises had been neglected during the war years and looked uninviting and dull to say the least. Again the irresistible urge to beautify came over me. But there seemed to be no way of paying even the smallest amount for such an undertaking.

My Bible companion book had told me that "Beauty is a thing of life, which dwells forever in the eternal Mind and reflects the charms of His goodness in expression, form, outline, and color" (*Science and Health*, p.247). This Mind, which I had learned to trust and listen to, I felt would point the way. By this time I had also begun to grasp the idea that there is a law of God which supports every normal human footstep for improvement and progress. This law of good, I found out later when I was asked by others to help them with business problems, can be applied

87

The Ultimate Freedom

to any legitimate business large or small. It is set forth most clearly in the Bible in the first three verses of the first Psalm:

> Blessed is the man that walketh not in the counsel of the ungodly, nor standeth in the way of sinners, nor sitteth in the seat of the scornful.
>
> But his delight is in the law of the Lord; and in his law doth he meditate day and night.
>
> And he shall be like a tree planted by the rivers of water, that bringeth forth his fruit in his season; his leaf also shall not wither; and whatsoever he doeth shall prosper.

Well, my attention was soon drawn to a row of black and white photograph enlargements mounted on the wall of the reception room. One of these was of a soldier drinking from a cup. I felt this photo enlargement had to go since the war was now over. It was replaced with an attractive photograph colored by a young woman of great artistic talent and ability.

Beauty and Business

The result was that the remaining black and white photographs in the display now appeared more unattractive and old-fashioned. These had to be replaced. And so it progressed! As one thing was renewed the next thing would cry out for beautifying. We had our own carpenter who made display stands for photographic work, and in his slack hours he would do the work of rejuvenating our premises. And money for this purpose became available as we went along. Soon the reception room was a glory of color and beauty, with new desks, built in seats for clients, and a large colored illuminated mural of an orchard in blossom. There were also beautiful arrangements of fresh flowers to feast the eyes on.

At that time it was impossible to move into other premises because of government building restrictions. Other businesses, as an aftermath of the war, found themselves in the same circumstances we had been in, with neglected showroom and office premises. This right idea, to beautify our own surroundings, had immediate consequences for good. A General Motors automobile agent came to see me about some

89

photographic work and expressed amazement at the transformation that had taken place. He asked if we could do the same for his premises. Suddenly we found ourselves with a brand-new lucrative type of work requiring the cooperation of builders, artists, designers, architects and planners in addition to our original staff. We received contracts to remodel banks, showrooms, tourist bureaus, milk bars, and even the interior of a train.

We now shipped the sections of murals, measuring ten by twenty feet (at that time considered very large), to other cities to be installed and colored by our personnel. The film business also grew. In the meantime, Mr. Ainsworth had regained his health and took an active part in the business of planning and designing while I continued to manage. And as our premises were gradually and entirely renewed, repainted and beautified, they served as an example for our newfound customers. And so the business of beautifying progressed and both we and our customers benefited.

Chapter Six

A NEW SPIRITUAL ADVENTURE

These were happy, productive years, but I knew God's plan for me was still unfolding when a friend of long standing called on me during business hours. He was on his way from New York to visit his family in Australia. This friend, George, held a responsible public information position with the United Nations and, on seeing how so many people of diverse talents were working so diligently together for the common good, asked how I would like to work on an even wider scale for the benefit of mankind.

He knew of my desire to see a better world come about because, when we were both still in our twenties, we had formed a non-political group of young people who would meet together to discuss how our world could be improved and made happier. With youthful enthusiasm we had

The Ultimate Freedom

called our discussion group, "The New World Movement," and George, who at that time was a radio announcer, had managed to get some of us on the air. This had drawn the attention of several notable people among whom was the famous novelist H.G. Wells who came to address our group. Unfortunately, we also drew the notice of members of the local Communist Party who infiltrated our group, and that was that. We disbanded! But both my friend and I retained our deep desire to do something for the benefit of humanity.

Now after a decade or more we met again, and spoke about our desire to see a better world and about our hopes that the United Nations would be a means to this end. George went on his way, but his visit left me with new thoughts that I might indeed work on an even broader scale in such an organization.

Before very long I received a telephone call from a man from the United Nations asking me to come to a hotel for an interview. He introduced himself as a talent scout for this organization and said the New York office had sent him to travel

A New Spiritual Adventure

around and look for likely candidates to fill posts there. This interview made me think that I would be offered something very soon. This, however, was not to be. Where I thought that my business experience now gained was a good basis from which to progress to work of greater benefit to mankind, God had a very different, but more excellent, plan.

My wife and I attended a Christian Science lecture one midday and were so uplifted and helped by what the lecturer had to say that we felt if we could only receive further instruction in Christian Science, with this man, our lives would be enormously enriched. The person who introduced him had informed the audience that the lecturer was also a practitioner and a teacher of Christian Science and that he resided in San Francisco.

From Sydney to San Francisco seemed like quite a leap, but we decided to take the first step. We wrote to the teacher and, after filling out applications, were accepted for class instruction. Then, during the months we had to wait for this instruction the idea came to us to sell our share in

The Ultimate Freedom

the business and arrange for ourselves and our teenage children to travel to Europe to visit my family in Holland after the class in San Francisco. However my planning didn't stop there. We could, I also figured out, stop over in New York and call in at the United Nations where I would surely be given a fine position. We would then take up residence in New York after our trip to Holland. Now this was the human outlining that so often leads to bitter disappointments.

The war had been over for about six years, but still no passenger ships had been placed back on the Australia-United States run. Some planes, however, were flying. So I booked passage with the airline, paid a deposit in local currency, and proceeded to sell our belongings. In the midst of all my preparations, I found there was no dollar exchange between the two countries. Only in rare cases could dollars be granted — medical studies and things to do for the government and similar projects — but not for the purpose of studying Christian Science.

And further, to obtain a visa I needed to show proof of support in the United States. I had

A New Spiritual Adventure

agreed to be in San Francisco on a certain date, and that date was rapidly approaching. When the government bank official told me the bad news about the dollar exchange, I responded with a trustful, "God will surely provide another way then." So convinced was I of the rightness of my desire to know more about this Science that I felt no obstacle could deprive me of this spiritual progress. The bank official was so taken by my assurance and trust in God that he asked for information about this way of thinking. I gave him a copy of *Science and Health*.

Now I must mention that as our belongings were being sold, I also sold my professional movie camera to a young movie maker. Some days after my visit to the bank he telephoned me. The conversation went something like this: "I hear you have booked passage to the United States of America. How would you like to go there free? Have your personal fare paid?" "Very much," I replied. "How would you like to spend a few days in Honolulu on your way over and stop at a fine hotel — free? How would you like a car and a chauffeur to drive you around the island — free?

The Ultimate Freedom

And how would you like a substantial check in dollars to cash in San Francisco?" By this time I'd had enough. "And what would you like for Christmas?" I asked him. But this is just how I came to study in San Francisco — with dollars to spare.

The questions were all quite serious. My friend had been commissioned to make a short travel film of a flight from Australia to San Francisco via Honolulu, and had discussed his project with the manager of the airline where I had booked my passage. When my friend mentioned he had just purchased a movie camera from me, it was suggested that I do the travel sequence in Honolulu and San Francisco with my own camera. And so it happened. I made the film, using my family as the actors, and the camera was shipped back on a return plane.

Why had all this come about? Because at the crucial moment when everything seemed to be going wrong, I had refused to listen to the discouraging arguments of the human mind. I needed only to listen to the encouraging assurances of the divine Mind — that God did love

A New Spiritual Adventure

me and would never deprive me of all I needed for my spiritual growth and human career. This experience showed me again how important it is to watch what is influencing us, and to be sure it is the divine Mind, God. Yes, each one of us can live the divine adventure. We can comprehend the All-in-all of good by resisting the human mind's limiting suggestions and instead letting God, the divine Mind, govern our thought and therefore our experience.

However, I was shortly to learn that prophesying can be risky and foolish, especially when one commits his life to God and then outlines what he thinks God ought to do. It's all in the Bible if we could only accept its guidance as humbly as a child: "Trust in the Lord with all thine heart; and lean not unto thine own understanding. In all thy ways acknowledge him, and he shall direct thy paths. Be not wise in thine own eyes:..." (Prov.3:5-7).

The Ultimate Freedom

The twelve days of instruction in Christian Science were an unforgettable experience. The things that stood out to me were the teacher's great love for Jesus and deep appreciation of Mary Baker Eddy. Also, the vastness of this Science dawned on me in this Class, but we had the teacher's loving assurance that we had all of eternity to work it out.

Jesus, it became more clear to me, was the most victorious, as well as the most Godlike man that ever walked our globe. He, it was so clearly explained, had triumphed over death, not submitted to it. This new concept that the Master had been his own healing practitioner while locked in the tomb, and that he had then reappeared to his disciples as the selfsame Jesus to show them (and us) the unreality of death, opened up for me a whole new and more Christian view of him. He showed death to be an illusion.

I could now understand why Jesus had said, "Our friend Lazarus sleepeth; but I go, that I may awake him out of sleep." According to the Gospel

Spiritual Instruction

of John (11:11-14), his disciples answered, "...Lord if he sleep, he shall do well. Howbeit Jesus spake of his death: but they thought that he had spoken of taking of rest in sleep. Then said Jesus unto them plainly, Lazarus is dead." The same thing about sleep was said about Jairus' daughter as recorded by Matthew (9:23-25). Jesus said this because of their lack of understanding of the unreality of death. "...when Jesus came into the ruler's house, and saw the minstrels and the people making a noise, he said unto them, Give place: for the maid is not dead, but sleepeth. And they laughed him to scorn. But when the people were put forth, he went in, and took her by the hand, and the maid arose."

Jesus also said, "Verily, verily, I say unto you, If a man keep my saying, he shall never see death" (John 8:51). Could a man, who made such a statement and who raised others from the belief in death, submit to death himself? No, Jesus overcame death. He proved death to be but a false concept that man lives in and dies out of a material body, while in reality he lives eternally in God, Spirit. Paul understood spiritual life when

The Ultimate Freedom

he said to the Athenians, "For in him we live, and move, and have our being; as certain also of your own poets have said, For we are also His offspring" (Acts 17:28).

I was now certain that it would be essential for all men and women to have a scientific statement of being to tell them who and what they really are so that this king of terrors — the belief that all must die — could be defeated. The Comforter, which Jesus promised, is understood by Christian Scientists to be Divine Science. And this Science as it is explained in *Science and Health with Key to the Scriptures* (p.468), does give us the following scientific statement of being:

> There is no life, truth, intelligence, nor substance in matter. All is infinite Mind and its infinite manifestation, for God is All-in-all. Spirit is immortal Truth; matter is mortal error. Spirit is the real and eternal; matter is the unreal and temporal. Spirit is God, and man is His image and likeness. Therefore man is not material; he is spiritual.

Spiritual Instruction

The teacher of the class pointed out that Jesus was prophesied about long before he appeared, and that Jesus in turn gave us a prophecy in a parable when he said: "The kingdom of heaven is like unto leaven, which a woman took, and hid in three measures of meal, till the whole was leavened" (Matt.13:33). The teacher explained that this prophecy is being fulfilled because the Science of Christ, which Mary Baker Eddy discovered, is leavening science, theology and medicine.

This class instruction also left me with the strong impression that most of my regenerating work to be done was not with the world, but with myself and that I had to, as Paul says, "...put off the old man with his deeds; and ...put on the new man, which is renewed in knowledge after the image of him that created him" (Col.3:9,10).

The Ultimate Freedom

A PHYSICAL HEALING

The opportunity to really work at this more earnestly came almost immediately. As planned, we made the United Nations Headquarters in New York our next stop enroute to Europe. Here I was told that, although my resume was looked upon very favorably, no post was available. I was stunned because, as I mentioned before, I had it all figured out how God was going to do things for me and I just could not understand what had gone wrong. Of course, nothing had gone wrong! It never does with God's plan for us. Instead an opportunity was provided me to rid my mental garden of some weeds in the form of self-will, self-righteousness, self-pity, etc., although I did not see this at that time. Neither did I know then that for the next two years I was going to have to do a lot of weeding!

During the flight from New York to Amsterdam, I recovered sufficiently from shock and disappointment to greet my dad and three brothers with some sense of joy. (My mother had

A Physical Healing

passed on some years before.) Although happy to see me, my family could not understand my recklessness in leaving one job while not having another firmly in hand. One brother even posed the somber question, "Do you realize that you may never get another job?" And, as none of my family had any knowledge of the Bible at that time, they looked upon my spiritual convictions with incredulity.

Added to this, family difficulties soon brought a flood of discord. So much so that my thinking became so clouded that all the good I had experienced in the past seemed to be wiped out, and I was left with a feeling of being a complete failure. This state of mind brought its bad effects in the form of a severe illness. Through a freak accident, I found myself in pretty bad shape. My left arm became completely useless, and I suffered excruciating pain throughout my left side. The symptoms became so alarming that the brother with whom we were staying became concerned for me and, without my knowledge, called a physician. When I became aware of what was happening, I heard this

The Ultimate Freedom

doctor's verdict that my arm would remain useless as there was no known cure for that condition. I did not accept this verdict since the many healings our family had already experienced had thoroughly convinced me of the restorative power of Christian Science. But self-pity, self-will, and resentment had by this time so gripped my thought that all I could think of was to get away and to get as close as possible to our ultimate goal — the United States.

We flew to Canada. Away from family discord, I found the pain in my arm and body subsided a great deal, though I was still not able to use my arm. Shock and self-condemnation also began to subside. To provide for our family both my wife and I took jobs, she as a saleswoman in a store selling jewelry and silver, and I selling automobiles. And the children went to school.

Turning wholeheartedly to working out the difficulty with my arm with the help of Christian Science, I took one specific idea from *Science and Health* and worked with it — that is, I put it into practice. It is found on page 428 and reads:

A Physical Healing

> To divest thought of false trusts and material evidences in order that the spiritual facts of being may appear, — this is the great attainment by means of which we shall sweep away the false and give place to the true. Thus we may establish in truth the temple, or body, 'whose builder and maker is God.'

In spite of the arm problem, I had been able to carry on my work without anyone noticing. Often I would park along the side of the road and work diligently with the above statements. I began to see that this was not really a physical condition but the result of my unhappy mental state. So I set about eliminating fear, self-pity, resentment, and discouragement, and replacing these with love, forgiveness (also forgiving myself), courage and trust in God. In a short time I was entirely healed. The power of God, of Truth and Love, was again beautifully experienced and a medical verdict proved invalid.

My wife and I now came to realize that our move to Canada had been precipitous and that it would have been wiser if we had gone the short

The Ultimate Freedom

distance from Holland to England where we had guidance to take our children to be educated. This guidance came from the president of a famed American college. He had advised us that it would be most advantageous for these high schoolers, because of their previous experience, education and upbringing, to continue their education in England.

So we set about retracing our steps humanly but advancing spiritually. With the healing of my arm came also a great desire to know more of the healing works done by Jesus and his disciples, so I set about reading the New Testament from beginning to end, also *Science and Health* and all of Mrs. Eddy's writings contained in *Prose Works*. The immediate result was that a number of people sought my metaphysical help, and these, in turn, would send others; and I became busy in this most rewarding work. I looked forward to meeting the requirements to advertise in *The Christian Science Journal*, a monthly publication containing, among other things, a worldwide listing of those participating full-time in the healing practice of Christian Science.

With the journey back to England, we had now used up practically all our money reserves. By the time we had settled in an apartment, we were depending wholly on what my wife earned in a broker's office and my earnings helping people solve their problems through Christian Science. All the while we were seeing results of our move to London in the good it did for our family. We were happy for our renewed willingness to depend wholly on God for guidance and to profit from our mistakes. And we found it true that "if you take the good out of your mistake, the mistake won't hurt you."

THE ECONOMY OF GRATITUDE

We were going along nicely meeting our obligations day by day, and I was enjoying my new and most satisfying healing profession when, suddenly, everything stopped. Day after day no one called on me. Toward the end of the week, I

The Ultimate Freedom

began to wonder what I was doing wrong. "Do something quickly. On Monday your rent is due. You need food for your family for the weekend. How could you do this to your wife and children?" So went the mental arguments fighting for supremacy in my thinking.

My family agreed that this problem should be solved in the best way we knew — that is, through prayer. I remembered that wonderful statement by Mary Baker Eddy,

> God gives you His spiritual ideas, and in turn, they give you daily supplies. Never ask for to-morrow: it is enough that divine Love is an ever-present help; and if you wait, never doubting, you will have all you need every moment (*Miscellaneous Writings,* p.307).

Friday came, and nothing happened. But I did suddenly get the thought that perhaps God was showing me something. This thought encouraged me no end. But Saturday morning came and now the mental suggestions poured in thick and fast: "Use your telephone and send an urgent telegram to your friends overseas and ask

The Economy of Gratitude

them to cable money." I refused to listen and I gave thanks for all the good I had received in the past. Yet the situation remained unchanged.

Then, looking out the window, I saw some of my neighbors loading up their cars to go for a weekend outing. Picnic baskets were brought out. Laughing children carried out tents and sporting equipment and helped to get ready for a happy time. Then suddenly it dawned on me! The truth that abundant life is wholly spiritual and present came to me most clearly, and I said, "Thank You, Father, that You are supplying Your children with all they need right now and always."

As soon as I had prayed this prayer of gratitude, the telephone rang and a wonderful thing happened. A voice at the other end of the line said, "I would like to tell you something, but please promise me that you will forgive me for what I am going to say." Rather startled, I replied, "I do not understand." I had only met this person casually and could see no earthly reason for her request. Well, after some hesitation, it came out. This is the gist of what she said: "All day yesterday something kept telling me to

The Ultimate Freedom

telephone you and offer you a check. But you seem to be so well off. You live at a very good address, and you and your family are very well dressed." Then the woman continued, "But now I'm telephoning you because this morning the thought became so persistent that the only way for me to end it was to call you."

Whatever possessed me, I don't know, but I responded with, "Oh, I don't need any money." Perhaps it was pride or another such devilish suggestion sneaking in that caused me to say this, but as soon as I had hung up the telephone, I realized that God was indeed showing me something. I managed to telephone back and said, "It was not true what I just told you. Please do what you felt impelled to do for me." "Oh, I am so glad," was the response. "That suggestion started again stronger than ever. So please come over and get the check, and you'll still be able to cash it before the bank closes."

I was offered an amount or double it. I took the smaller amount which was enough to meet the rent and food for the weekend. The woman's parting words were, "There are no strings attached to this. I have more money than I can use. Please accept it with my gratitude for God having used me."

From that day the calls for help came again, and ever since then I have enjoyed ample supply. I learned that supply truly comes from God, that it may come <u>through</u> people but not <u>from</u> people — sick people or well people. So our real need is always to entertain in consciousness the right spiritual ideas, which, in turn, give us our daily supply. And we can always do this by looking to God, the all-knowing Mind, for our help.

Chapter Seven

THE UNITED NATIONS

Our experiences living in London were valuable ones. We also gained a good insight into the British character which in itself is an education in law-abiding behavior, good sportsmanship in human relations, and uncomplaining, dogged courage under trying circumstances.

My dear friend George, who came to see me in Australia some years before and had recommended me to the United Nations, was transferred from New York to head the United Nations Office in London. Our families had many happy times together. However, my longing to live in the United States persisted, and I still hoped that in some way this dream would be realized.

Then one day it happened! George telephoned me saying that the United Nations had been looking for me and, not being able to locate me, had called him to find out if he knew my whereabouts. I was asked to go to the United Nations Children's Fund (UNICEF) office in London as a post was now available for me. Interestingly, I was informed there that the reason a post had not been offered before was that only now a sufficiently high one had become available. This was in the form of Assistant Director of Public Information for UNICEF in New York.

To accept this position would mean putting on hold my desire to advertise and to continue in the full-time practice of Christian Science. But evidently there was more for me to learn about the widest and highest way for me to help mankind, and the means for doing this. A family council was held, and it was unanimously decided that I should accept this offer. My wife's parents, who just at this time had come from Australia to England, would live in our apartment with our teenagers until we could sort things out.

I was asked to sign a two-year contract and was told that it would take me one year to understand the working of the various agencies

The United Nations

and their intertwined operations. How many hundreds of years, I wondered, would it take for such people as Europeans, Africans, and people from India (to name a few) to find a common basis from which to think, act, and work together harmoniously. While being grateful that the nations of the world were inching somewhat in the right direction, it now became clear to me that my thinking would have to proceed more and more along spiritual lines if I were to fill my proper niche in the scheme of things.

Not long after taking up my post, I was asked to go to Greece and Africa with a cameraman and make some films to be shown to the representatives of the various nations who contributed to the United Nations Children's Fund. This assignment, to me, was an opportunity to get further education in understanding mankind's hopes and aspirations as well as problems, a knowledge which would later stand me in good stead.

My African experience was especially interesting and brought me into contact with people who very seldom see a white man. A people both lovable and hospitable. Yes, Africa has much to teach us in the way of love for one another. I will never forget the tenderness I saw when a man said goodbye to his wife as she joined our group to be taken by a Swiss doctor to a hospital. There was no emotional scene, but just the most tender affection as he pressed some money into her hand and their faces touched. After my experiences in that country how could I ever think more or less of any man or woman for living in a palace or a hut in the depths of equatorial Africa.

However, as my work continued I witnessed within the United Nations almost daily conflicts of interest even among people of the same nationality. It became evident that an understanding of and an obedience to the true power which governs the universe should be put into practice. Then the nations of the world could find the peace and well-being they so earnestly desired.

My two years with the United Nations proved to be quite an education in human relations. It provided an overview of people of various nationalities, with their many differing customs and beliefs, all endeavoring to harmonize with each other to achieve an ideal — peace and prosperity for everyone through the unifying of the nations. But I saw that this world-peace ideal could not be achieved on merely a human or unspiritual basis.

Turning to my textbooks, the Bible and *Science and Health*, I searched for the spiritual guidance which would apply directly to solving the social, political and war problems facing the United Nations. This is what I found in my companion book to the Bible:

> One infinite God, good, unifies men and nations; constitutes the brotherhood of man; ends wars; fulfils the Scripture, 'Love thy neighbor as thyself;' annihilates pagan and Christian idolatry, — whatever is wrong in social, civil, criminal, political, and religious codes; equalizes the sexes; annuls the curse on man, and leaves nothing that can sin, suffer, be punished, or destroyed (*Science and Health*, p.340).

The Ultimate Freedom

It seemed that these words, written over a hundred years ago, applied directly to what the United Nations was trying to accomplish.

Why, here was a blueprint for the United Nations to follow!

Epilogue

What John Wyndham perceived as a blueprint for the United Nations may not be written on the walls of the nations' capital cities, but he certainly wrote it in the hearts of the many whose lives he touched. He kept the promise made in the prison camp, — to live his life to serve God.

After serving two years with the United Nations, he made his home in Los Angeles and devoted 21 years to the healing practice of Christian Science. During this period he also became an authorized teacher of this subject.

However, if John Wyndham thought his travels were over they were really only about to begin, for in 1968 he was appointed to lecture. In this capacity he spoke almost nightly in the United States for nine months of the year, traveling by car from city to city. His ten years of lecture tours also took him to Australia, Canada, England, Europe and Africa, speaking to audiences in English, Dutch, German and Afrikaans.

There was a statement included in one of John Wyndham's lectures that groups, large or small, always received with joy. When he delivered this lecture in an auditorium packed with five thousand people, the audience spontaneously broke into applause at this point.

Holding up three fingers, he would vigorously proclaim: "There are three things God will not let you have. They are sin, sickness and death." Then spreading his arms out wide he would fairly shout: "All the rest, you can have!" Certainly most of us would agree that this is the ultimate freedom.

A.W.L.